STRUCTURING YOUR NOVEL

How to Structure and Outline Your Story to Write an Exceptional Novel

Richard England

CLAIM YOUR FREE BONUS GUIDE!

Want to know how to write outstanding characters for your novel?

Now that you have "Structuring Your Novel", it's time to learn how to write outstanding characters in for your story.

Discover key secrets for writing outstanding characters in this FREE bonus three step guide.

"This guide totally unlocked my ability to write outstanding characters for my novel."

GET YOUR FREE COPY OF THIS THREE STEP GUIDE HERE BY GOING TO THIS ADDRESS:

www.bit.ly/Claim-My-Free-Guide

Table of Contents

Introduction

I would like to first thank you for purchasing this book, "Structuring Your Novel". Make sure you also claim the Free gift bonus I have for you as well as a thank you for your support and purchase.

In this book i'm going to cover key strategies and techniques in regards to How to Structure and Outline Your Story to Write an Exceptional Novel. These strategies I cover in this book are surprisingly overlooked, and misunderstood by many writers. However, the strategies in this book are ones that lead to writing outstanding stories that readers love. Not only will these strategies help you in the journey of writing an exceptional story, but they will also make the whole writing process much better. These strategies also help to make the writing process so much easier, faster, and more enjoyable for many authors as well.

In this book i'm going to walk you through the exact techniques of how to structure and outline your story, in order to write a

compelling story that really works. These techniques will help you to write a story that is captivating, and compelling to your readers, and that really shines. These techniques will help to element the roadblocks encountered in the writing process, in turn making it much easier to write an exceptional story. Though I cannot guarantee that if these techniques are followed that you will be able to write a bestselling story, I can say that by following these writing craft techniques you can have a much better chance. The techniques covered in this book are the exact writing craft techniques that many bestselling novel authors use to write their bestselling stories.

When these structuring and outlining techniques are used in the novel writing process the whole process for many becomes more exciting, effective, easier, and liberating. I want to encourage you to really apply and test out every technique that I cover in this book for your story and novel. Really give it your all to apply what you learn and just try it. Once you have really implemented and tried everything you will really discover more of what really works for you in the whole writing process and what does not. At the end of the day it's all about helping you to improve your writing craft in order to write better stories for yourself and your readers. So feel completely free after you have tried all the different techniques to use what works for you, and discard what does not. I hope that you enjoy the journey of structuring your novel.

Richard England

Chapter 1: To Structure or Not To Structure

The main goal is to write a great story that you and your readers love. In this first chapter of Structuring Your Novel, we are going to first look into why structuring your novel is so important as well as the benefits it provides. We also going to discuss how not having a structure for your novel can just cause problems for you as a writer and storyteller. Not having a structure for your novel can cause large loss of time, mistakes, broken story elements, frustration, and a good amount of work that has to be rewritten and thrown in the trash at the end the day to fix what didn't work. Let's dive into looking at these elements and benefits of why structuring your novel is so important.

When you mention beginning a novel or new series with structuring, some writers may be against the idea before they really dive in and try it. In fact, I was actually one of those people. My thoughts were initially that writing is meant to be creative, that I should be able to just jump into my new world not knowing what will happen for sure, or where things will go. I thought I could just begin the adventure of writing to see and watch it play out effectively right before my eyes as I put the story to paper, writing it out as the wonderful creative spontaneous flow would just come. The very idea of even starting the creative process with a structure by structuring my novel was offensive to my soul as a beginning writer. This was until I actually learned more about the importance and benefits of structuring, and what it really provided for me as the writer and to the story and novel overall. What I also found is that the create from scratch as you go flow gardening method just did not work for me. I continued to have and run into problems in what I was writing and could not make things go or fit together in a way that worked with my writing, issues with the creation of my plot, chapters, characters, scenes, and so on. I had to find another way, another effective approach to writing that made writing and creating a great story novel easier and more effective for me.

One of the main things I discovered about writing from the place of "create as you go" method, and not really having a good foundational structure for my novel, is that if I just started writing to create "naturally" I would get confused often as well. I would get confused about the direction of the plot and scene's that I was writing, as well as how that will work well with the main plot, subplots, and characters in my story. I would get hung with different elements in the scene's of my characters interactions, and personalities. All these problems just caused much frustration to the writing process for me.

By not having a good starting structure to write from I found that I would just end up with a good amount of wasted time and work, through making mistakes with the story development, scenes, character interactions, etc. I would have to redo a bunch of the writing, frankly because of silly things that I really should have worked out before I even started to write. Now this is me and coming from my experience, but I have found that many famous best selling authors actually promote and teach structuring your novel for these very reasons and benefits as well. At the end of the day, your novel is your novel, and you are free to write any way you choose to if it works well for you. I am just here to share how myself and many best selling authors avoid many of potential problems with the development and writing of novels, as well as just making the whole writing process so much easier and fluid for us.

To discuss some other benefits of structuring your novel from what I have found, is that without structure certain events, interactions, and other things just happen sometimes without being a result of something which can sometimes lose the attention of the reader in the progression of the story. Remember that one of the main goals of a great story is to continually captivate the reader's attention because the moment they lose interest or attention in the current direction of the story can be the moment they decide to stop reading a particular novel. And in today's society, readers are having less and less attention span to stay engaged through elements of a story that just doesn't effectively grip their attention, make sense, or if progression seems too slow or too much for them. Having a good structure for your novel will also ensure that nothing just happens without a purpose in your story, and every thing that occurs is beneficial for the development of the progression of your overall story and character development.

Structuring your novel the right way will make sure you write your novel in such a way that will keep your the attention of your readers, as well as keep them engaged with your novel. Having a good structure will mean that you will have an easier time of writing a great story that will captivate your readers, and that you and your readers will love.

At the end of the day structuring your novel helps you write a story that works, and works well every single time that you sit down at your desk to write. It helps us to not venture into our stories totally or partially blind, and gives us a guiding structure to write a great effective story. Once you understand this process I will cover on structuring your novel, it is also so simple. Structuring your novel just gives you power over your story; you truly get to be the master and creator of your story instead of it's slave. Structuring your novel is the key to a great fluid story that works so well. Now let's dive into the next chapter of where to begin.

Chapter 2: Where to Begin

Brainstorming And Mining Out Your Premise

The first structuring element and skill that we are going to tackle is brainstorming, mining out, and creating the premise for your novel. If you were like me when I first approached the task of structuring and outlining was just confusion as to how to even begin. I remember staring down at a piece of paper trying to think of how to convey what was in my heart and head, and stick it down on that paper, and I had no idea of what to do. Then I found the key that really unlocked the structuring and outlining process for me, and that was that in order to create a structure and outline you must first have a premise for your novel. A basic premise is the very cornerstone of your novel. Let's discuss exactly how to create a great premise for your novel.

Let's start with a simple technique that has helped me to generate a premise effectively for novels premise. The goal here is the use this technique to generate a premise for your novel, that you can then use to generate an outline.

The Setting

For the first step of that process which is establishing your novel's "Setting". Your setting is what compasses everything that makes your novel a part of whatever genre that it is in. So for example if your series is the Fantasy genre you now need to establish the setting for things: magic, dragons, creature types, character race and class types, kingdoms, castles, etc. And whatever other things your world may consist of. You want to be able to get a sense of what other intellectual property or "IP" novel that your novel is most similar to. What I mean by this is selecting another author's published and success story novel in your genre for this IP reference. For example if you have a specific fantasy book in mind that is most closely similar to the world and setting that you are trying to create, then you can choose that as your reference IP novel. This IP reference is only going to be used as a helpful reference foundational point, you are not going to copy or clone this work or what you pick. You can just use this reference to help as a starting point, to help you define what you are really writing. The IP you select does not have to be and should not be exactly like your novel, but just the closest world setting resemblance to help assist you as a reference.

Once you pick another author's novel as your IP that is most closely similar to the setting of your novel, you can use this author's novel to help inform your ideas of how your plot is going to develop. Just by picking another novel that is somewhat similar to your setting, and similar to what you want to write is going to enable you to build a great setting for your novel. This is especially helpful if you ever get stuck in the creation process of your setting. You should figure out what you are going to write and what it is most like, and whenever you have a question about how your world or setting works your default can then be to just go to your reference the IP novel you selected. If you ever get stuck in the process with an element of how something will work in your novel and setting you can just say, for now it works like it does in "X" novel or whatever that novel IP is that you have selected. You can then refine that more later and make it more of your own, but for now you just want a starting point and this technique really helps to provide that.

The Protagonist

For brainstorming and mining out the next part of your premise we are going to establish some key things for your "lead" or "protagonist" if you will. This would be the person or character that is ultimately going to oppose your antagonist in your novel, and this is the person who has the most to lose throughout the course of your novel. So now we need to establish some simple elements to start off with for your lead or protagonist. Simple elements that you need to now establish for your lead come down to:

1. Who is your protagonist and what is his/her gender?

2. What is his or her name?

3. What is their age within your current

world setting?

4. What is their current position, place, and what is the protagonists current whereabouts within your worlds society or setting?

As an example for defining the beginning and foundational protagonist elements and continuing with my fantasy example it will look something like this next example. For the first and second points let's say that our protagonist is a male Elf, and his name is Adran. For the third protagonist element let's say that Adran is one thousand and ten years old, and that elves in this world can live to be as much as three thousand years old. The reason defining age can be important is because how old you see your character's within a given world can have a great impact on the development and current personality of the character. This at least gives us a starting element reference point on understanding the protagonist beginning point a little better. For the fourth element of the protagonist, let's say that Adran is from the forest kingdom of Alion, and he is actually the elven King's son, and is head over all the Alion elven guard.

The Antagonist

Once you have that setting, then let's now move onto one of the most important parts that you will define which is the antagonist. This is the villain if you will, the person/people, being, force, or situation that is going to go against your lead character or characters in your novel. We don't need to determine everything about your antagonist here, but we do need to establish some basic elements. These elements and characteristics that we need to establish here really come down to four key elements, which are things such as:

1. Who or what is the antagonist?

2. What is the antagonist(s) name?

3. What is the antagonist's goal that they are seeking to achieve?

4. What is some history or event(s) in your world that is playing into your

antagonist's ultimate goal and desire?

For starting out and beginning here this is really all that you need to know about your antagonist because your antagonist will be fleshed out more in depth throughout the process of outlining your novel. In the beginning you just need a few sentences of who the person or thing is that is going to serve as the antagonist in your novel and story.

To give an example of this let's say that I am writing a fantasy novel, and in my fantasy story I want to create an antagonist who is a great dark lord, and this dark lord is named "Synok". "Synok's" goal and desire is to completely gain lordship over all the world, and annihilate all that oppose him and his goal. For the fourth element here is to write out any foundational points any history or event(s) that make up who your antagonist is currently. An example of this could be as basic as, "Synok" has been exiled for the last 100 years and is now returning. If you have other history in mind you can also go further in depth with your backstory, but this can also be really basic for now.

As you can see this is a very simple way to establish some basic but very important main key points for the antagonist in your novel. We do not need to go too in depth, keep it simple. This should be a very high level view here, and then you will really drill down into this and flesh it out more later.

The Ending Point

Now that we have established the foundational elements of your setting, antagonist, and protagonist for your novel, we now have the cornerstones built. The last two foundational things that we need next are an ending, and a starting point. Now let's dive into the elements of each of these that we need to now mine out for our novel's premise.

The importance of now establishing an ending helps us to ultimate know and determine where the story of your novel is ultimately going to end up. Like I have said previously for other elements this does not have to be all fleshed out you will get to that later as you develop your novel more. The goal here is to just establish the simple main ending elements of your novel's story. This helps us to have a road map of where the story and novel is ultimately going so that we have a point of reference to measure everything else against, which helps us stay honest of whether an element of our story, outline, writing, and scenes for example are actually helping the novel and story to progress to the ultimate ending. This helps us to know that every aspect of our novel is indeed adding to and not taking away from the progression of the overall story. Have you ever hear the famous quote by Stephen Covey, "begin with the end in mind"? This is the concept of if you want to make sure that where you end up is actually where you want and desire to be, you must first begin with the end in mind and know where you are going.

What we will now look at is the elements we need to establish for the ending premise. Again this is just a high level general idea and vision of where the novel story is ultimately going and ending. The fine details will be established more later on. Let's brainstorm and establish the simple, high level elements for the ending, which consist of the following two general elements:

1. What is the basic and general setting for this ending?

2. Where and how will the protagonist or hero emerge to face the antagonist and the antagonists agenda in the end of your novel's story?

For an example, and continuing with the fantasy scenario we have been using so far, we will now give examples for the ending two elements we just discussed. For the first element, we will say that the dark lord Synok is very close to, and about to accomplish his ultimate goal and desire of claiming lordship over all the world, and annihilating all the good Kingdom's and people that oppose him. Which in turn will cause darkness and evil to spread, rule and reign throughout the entire world. Our protagonist hero Elf Adran is really the only one who has the chance to stop Synok from achieving his goal.

For the second ending element we will say that Adran, our protagonist, comes to face the dark lord Synok face to face in order to attempt to prevent Synok from overcoming and annihilating all that oppose him throughout the world. Thus Adran is attempting to prevent evil and darkness from spreading and reigning over the world.

You can see that this is very general and high level view, and not very well defined. However, we now have a general idea of the ending and where we are ultimately going with the story. Now that we have the general idea for the ending in mind, we can work backwards from that and now look for a starting point for the novel's story. We now know some general but key foundational elements of the novel.

The Starting Point

We have now established and know what our antagonist and protagonist want, what the general loose ending is, now we can brainstorm and work backwards to determine where they will start.

In order to figure out the starting point and now that we have a good foundational understanding of the premise, as well as have the general ending defined we can now work backwards from there to define a good starting point. To define a good starting point for your protagonist and antagonist work backwards from the ending point since we know where we are ultimately going. Now is the time to brainstorm different starting point ideas that really make sense for your novel's plot and story. Make sure that you enjoy and are excited about writing whatever you come up with here for your novel's story as a starting point. If you are not excited about it, we cannot expect the reader to be. There are the two elements for you to define here:

1. Where does your protagonist start in your story?

2. Where does your antagonist start in your story?

For the starting point example we will say that Adran our lead protagonist will begin the story as he heads to the western watchguard tower of the forest kingdom of Alion to check and meet which his head chief of the guard there to discuss the western watch and guard of Alion. Adran's starting point is in the main fortress Kingdom of Alion in the center of the forest and gathering supplies for his journey to the western tower. For the second element of the antagonist starting point, we will say that Synok the dark lord is in the far north and still in the process of preparing for his return. Again the general elements high view is what we are determining here, as we will flesh out more of the specific details later.

Writing Your Synopsis

Now that we have determined all these elements of our novel's premise, and that we have both a general ending point and a starting point for both our protagonist lead and antagonist we can build our way forward back up to that ending we defined. Going from here we know that everything that we write is going to have to touch on making sense with that beginning point, and end point. If we ever have any questions about what that in between story progression is going to be, we will now use the setting, the antagonist, and the protagonist lead to flesh that out.

There is one final step that we need to do here when building and defining our premise, and that is to take the defined elements from the process above for our story and write a synopsis. This first synopsis should be maybe a paragraph or so using the above information elements we have already defined for the novel's premise. As you write the synopsis continue to ask yourself the question "why?" on each line element that you write, to help you further clarify and your story. This is where you want to question everything, and write down the answers to the questions. This will really help in further mining out this portion to get it the way you want it, and in a way that works well for your story. A few things to ask yourself here are;

- Why is the protagonist lead doing what he or she is doing?

- Why is the antagonist or villain doing what he or she is doing?

You can now use these answers that you come up as well as the other elements you have defined as your notes to write a cast of "Characters" list that come to mind. As you think about your story write down a list of any other potential characters, as well as possible names that come to mind that could fit well into your novel. You can continually now be evolving this organically as you work on structuring, your plot, and the rest of the things that we will cover in this book.

As you continue to write your synopsis and ask yourself "why?" on each element of your story, document the answers to those questions. You should then be developing a notepad of a list of questions and answers to your story that help it evolve into a more specific vision for your story than the general one we defined above. It is totally okay, if you don't yet have the answers to everything. Don't stress out, this is your story, and at the end of the day you can do what works and is enjoyable for you. At the end of the day remember, one of the great keys to a successful story for a novel is for the author to create and write a story that they themselves love and would love to read.

Here are some questions that can be very helpful to ask here:

- Why do these specific characters know each other?

- What is there relationship and attitude towards one another?

- What are each of the characters goals and desires?

- How could each of them mess up?

- What each of their goals?

- What our each character's current skills and capabilities?

- What are their personalities like?

- How long before our antagonist is going to return?

- What does our antagonist have left to do before he can return, or what needs to happen?

These are just a few examples of some good questions to ask yourself that can get you started, and by you asking one question it will then just lead to other questions that you can ask and work out the answers. When you are done answering and mining out all of these questions, what you are going to now do is rewrite your 2nd draft of your synopsis based on all of this new information that has been answered and defined for your novel's story.

If you have any ideas or vision for your world this can be a great time to also do some world building but asking yourself questions about your world by answering those questions for yourself . Remember now that you have a foundational framework for your premise and anything you come up with must make sense to fit into what you have already defined.

The second synopsis version should end up being much longer than your first one. Having this, much more detailed synopsis, will make the process of outlining your novel much easier. Then what you can do is to even take the second synopsis version and do the process again of asking and answering more and more questions which lead to more questions and inevitably lead to more answers. This will create the third version of your synopsis. Then use all of the information to build a third, longer and more detailed version of the synopsis which will give us even more information for outlining our novel and will make it that much more effortless.

Don't rush yourself with this process, you have to let yourself really work through all of it. One piece of advice I would suggest here is just take all the pressure off yourself. You have nothing to lose but everything to gain. Have fun with this process! Enjoy this process of developing the premise for your new novel, how exciting is this?! It is such a wonderful and amazing journey and adventure to write a novel and story, so just be patient with yourself and enjoy it as you have fun with the process. Remember that sometimes in this whole premise building and brainstorming process you just have to set things down for a day or two and just think and day dream about it as you go about your normal day and then come back to it later to help have a refreshed new energy and perspective on things. Do not assume that you are going to sit down for an hour and completely have it all planned and defined. And don't try to be perfect because perfection is not real and is an illusion anyways. depending on the story and novel, or even series that you are trying to build here this process could take you some time and sessions of a few days, a few weeks, or depending on the depth of your world and story or due to the time that you have to work on it potentially even longer. Don't rush, just go at your own pace that you enjoy. I do suggest to try and do at least a little bit each day to work on refining this process skill, and craft.

I hope you have enjoyed this development process and hope that it really helps you by providing some tools on crafting a great beginning point and foundation for you to build from when structuring your novel. You can use this process to define and build your novel's premise to help give good foundation of where to begin structuring your novel.

I want to reiterate after covering the

techniques in this chapter that when it comes to writing your novel it is your world, your story, and your novel, and you can test out different techniques and skills that may really help you in planning, creating, and writing your novel. However, if you still find that you enjoy the invent as you go method more, or any other technique then do that. Do what works best for you, and what you enjoy and get the most fulfillment from. In this book I am just sharing some skills and techniques that have really helped me and many successful authors in the novel writing process. I am sharing things that have helped many of us to avoid certain mistakes and write stories that actually work for us, and write them more efficiently and fluidly in the process. Just remember that when it comes to writing, there are no hard and fast rules at the end of the day, and you get to decide as the writer what you want to do.

Chapter 3: Structuring And Plotting

In this chapter I want to take some time to cover the most important aspects to plotting your novel and the main plotting keys, and why they are important. When it comes to plotting, the number one, and most important thing about plotting is that you have to know where you are ultimately going. You have got to have a place and destination that you are going to with your story, and where you are ultimately ending up. In saying that, you do not have to know every single detail of the journey along the way, but you do have to know how your novel is going to end, why is it going to end that way, and what positions are your characters going to be in when they get to the end. If you have ever driven anywhere without knowing where you are ultimately trying to end up, you know of the possibility that you may find yourself making all kinds of mistakes and wrong turns in the process.

Ultimately, lack of directions to your endpoint can just cause you to waste a bunch of time and effort, as well as cause frustration. The same goes for the process of writing a novel, that if you know the endpoint and where you are ultimately trying to end up, then the journey of getting there is going to be much easier for you as the writer. This is exactly where plotting your novel comes into play. Now let's really dive into how to plot your novel.

Plotting

Plot Arcs And The Three Act Story Structure Model

For plotting and story structure we are going to be discussing something called the "Three Act Story Structure", or "The Three Act Model" which is very commonly used for story and plot structuring among novel and fiction writers. We are going to dive in and take a deeper look into this model and structure, and how it works. This method is really going to help you with structuring your novel's plot and story. When it comes to the three act story structure there are several phases as to how it works.

For the three act story structure the story starts with the "exposition", and then some sort of conflict or what the model calls the "inciting incident", which is something that is interrupting the lead or protagonists world. From there you have rising tension or "rising action" in the story until you get to the Climax of the novel. After this, the story has the "falling action" of everything wrapping up for the ending of the story called the "resolution", and then story ends. This structure is considered the plot archetype or "plot arc", and is considered the "main plot arc" in a story. I have actually made and put a plot diagram just below displaying this plot and story structure, so take a look at it for reference, as everything is going to be built around this.

PLOT DIAGRAM

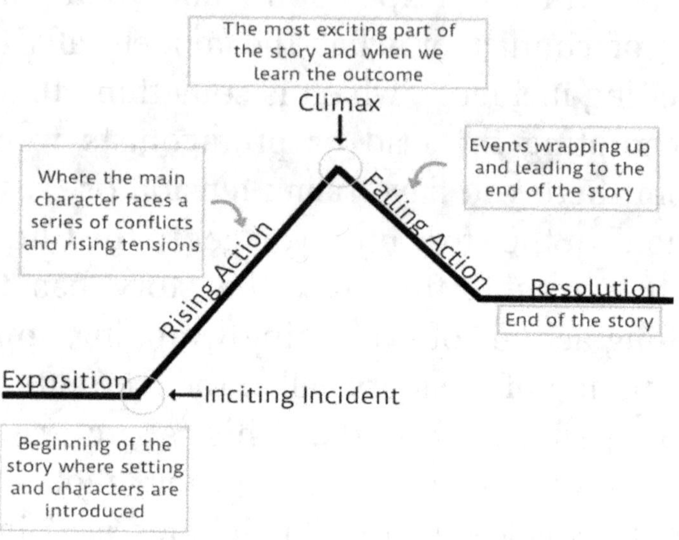

As you can see in the plot diagram, this shows us the flow of plot that we can now use to build everything in our story around. For the next part we will discuss how everything is broken down into the three act structure. And in the next few chapters we will take a deeper look into each of the act structures as well. The plot and story structure for a novel often consists of a main plot, as well as the subplots however many there maybe. You will have the main story plot that is the flow of the main premise from the starting point of your novel to the ultimate climax of your story, and then the ending. This main flow is what I am referring to in regards to the main plot. For the subplots of your novel you can have many different ones that go along working with the main plot, but an example of a subplot would be a growing relationship between the main character and another characters in your novel for example. There could be several subplots intertwined with different character relationships, or places that ultimately progress with and tie into the main plot. You can use the subplot for this to see how the relationships in your novel evolve throughout your story plot. We can have more clarity on this by asking questions like, "Where does the relationship start?", "Where does it end?", "And how does it get there?".

With this structure each plot in your novel will need to have a beginning, a middle, and an end. So really with this plotting and structure you are taking your novel premise, story, characters, world, and so on, that you have established, and you can then put these dots down along the plot. By using plotting and story structure you are connecting those dots in the plot, and we will look at exactly how to do this. This is the point of the plot arcs that we are going to dive into in the next few chapters for structuring your novel. Now take a look at the plot diagram for three acts structure that I have made and put below. This contains the three phases of the beginning, the middle, and the end of a plot which are the three separate acts of the story structure.

PLOT DIAGRAM FOR THREE ACTS

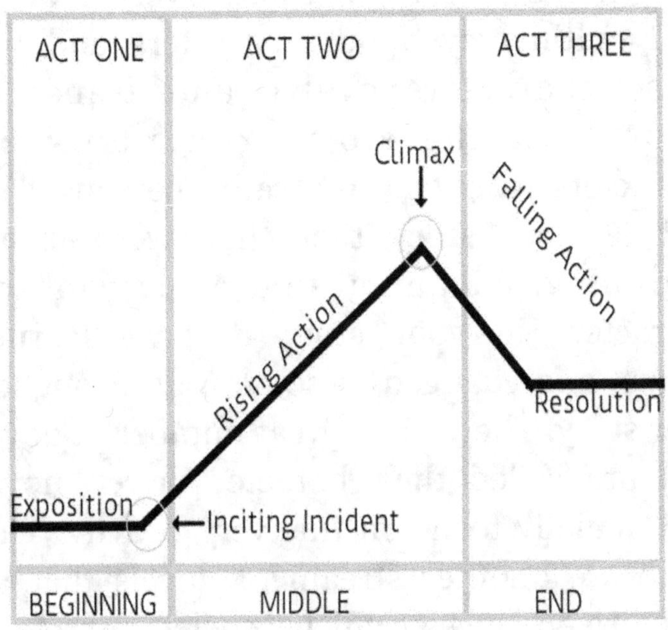

Character Arcs

Now let's look into the difference between plot and character arcs, because every story is really ultimately about characters and how those characters evolve and transform throughout the story. You want your characters to not be the same person at the end of your story that they were in the beginning. Meaning that you want the characters in your story to have learned, grown, and changed in some way throughout your story. There are a great number of novels that are called the Character driven novels that actually focus on this very heavily. Then there are another stream of novels that are plot driven novels which is what myself, as well as many authors use instead. This is what we are discussing here in these chapters. The plot driven novel structure is more about the events that are actually occuring in the story. Our characters are going to grow and evolve within our story and plot, and they really need to do this. However, the characters growing and evolving is not the focal point of the story and main plot itself even though they are a large part of it.

When you are building this framework for your novel, you can take a more plot based approach using this method, and then tying your characters into that. Don't misunderstand what we are saying here though, it is still vital and very important to have great characters, and to allow them to grow and evolve as the plot and story progresses. It really just comes down to a choice of what you are starting with, and starting with the plot and premise what I am suggesting and discussing in this book. For your novel it really comes down to if you want a plot driven, or character driven story. Either way is right and correct, it really comes down to more of what kind of writer you are and which method really works best for you as a writer. However, there is no real way to know that until you dive in and try the three act plotting structure approach to see how well it works for you. And when we are saying that a novel story is plot driven, this does not mean that it doesn't have character driven aspects throughout the story as well. It also does not mean that within your structure you cannot be creative and allow the story to grow organically. I have found this structure allows and enables my story to more easily grow organically and well. This plot driven method is just really is referring to our main flow and progression of our story throughout the novel.

A great little case study to do here (if you really want to), is to look at your favorite novels, as well as the best selling novels in your particular genre that you are wanting to write in. Look at very successful novels as well that are similar to the novel story setting genre that you are going to be writing with your novel. Then dive in and do some research on the internet as to if those novels are considered mainly plot driven, or character driven novels. What I found by doing this process myself was that all of my favorite novels, and ones mainly read were all mainly considered plot driven. I found that the famous best selling novels in my genre from famous authors were novels in which the authors themselves had a plot driven approach to their writing.

At the end of the day, you need to write whichever story type you really like, enjoy, and that works best for you as a writer. Plot-driven versus Character-driven really doesn't make that much of a difference standing on its own, it really is all about what works best for you and your novel. If you make sure to skillfully craft a story that has amazing characters, great character development throughout the progression of the plot, as well as a strong plot for the story, then goal accomplished.

Using Your Premise To Develop Plot And Story Arcs

We will now begin this portion of structuring your novel with using your premise now in order to develop your plot and story arcs. The first step in this process is to now take a look at the latest version of your premise synopsis that you have created. Then using the synopsis to define the major elements of what is going on in the story. What are the things here that are the most important to the reader? What needs to be resolved by the end? We need to know what the goal is here is to find the broad plot arcs that you need to define now through using your created and written premise synopsis.

An example here is that you may see in the synopsis that you have written out a relationship between two characters that really needs to be fleshed out more now for example. So what we are going to do is take that relationship between two characters that you see and plot it out. We are going to look at the relationship here between two characters which we need to flesh out and ask ourselves "where is plot a beginning point?", "where is an ending point?". Next we are then going to look at what may happen in the middle to get from the beginning to the ending point. You just need to determine the beginning, the ending, and then this allows us to plot out what authors call the "beats" in this particular plot in the middle of that beginning and end. This can and will be very loosely defined usually here because it's not the main plot.

Beats in the plot are not usually very obvious. Beats for example within the character arcs are like parts of a broken down scene in which mark the moments of relationship changes, or mood changes that can occur between two characters in a particular scene. The term "beats" can also be used to reference larger scale changes throughout the plot. That's about all that we are going to say on beats, as we will dive into scene structure soon. So you can note this but don't really worry too much about it.

Now that we have our premise synopsis and have been through the above methods, we our going to develop our main plot arc. With this step we are basically just taking our premise synopsis and rewriting it as the main plot arc. This main plot arc, is not written for the reader. This main plot arc is written for your as the author to be able to write and see all the main elements of your plot. What this is going to allow us to do as the author is to form the three act structure that we are going to dive into more in the next chapter. Once you do this and take the time to write out all the specific parts of your main plot, this will allow you to look at specific parts more closely. Things like the inciting incident, and conflict that we briefly mentioned, are going to be pulled from what we are really creating here. This covers the foundation of plot arcs.

For the character arcs, your character arcs need to be given a foundation as well now. When just starting your novel these can be a little more shallow than they really end up being. This will evolve more as you go along the way of the plot and story. However, they still need to be there, and we are just laying a bit of a foundation and beginning for them. Lets now explore this and discuss this a bit, as well as take our example fantasy character Adran, and use him as an example of what his character arc could be.

We are going to say for this example that in the beginning of the book Adran's comfort zone is to continue serving his kingdom of Alion as head of the Guard under his father, and his King's command. He is faithful, and loyal to his father who is King, and their elven forest kingdom of Alion. He doesn't really have any desire for any change of his current life or senario. However, he is the heir to the elven kingship after his father is gone. Adran has no desire or interest to rule however, and feels that obligation weighing on his heart. By the end of the book he is going to have been forced to venture out of his kingdom as he is going to discover at some point that he is indeed the only one who has the chance to stop the villain antagonist named Synok. His father whom he loves dearly, end's up being killed by Synok's main leader which because of his heirship by default makes him become the new King of Alion. This happens way before Adran expected that this responsibility could possibly could potentially take place. Therefore, Adran is going to have to grow as a character to realize that he is the only hope for the realm to have a chance against the dark lord, and he must rise to this occasion. So this is Adran's beginning character arc.

The next step is now to take each character who is apart of the main plot arc that has been defined and develop each one's character arc like this example. We can see with the character arc example that this consists of a foundational beginning point, ending point, and then using those to determine the middle point or change or conflict that we are going to be seeing in that character throughout the middle. This gives us a greater foundation as we write different scenes, to help us stay true to who the character is, where they are ultimately going, as well as with the main plot.

What will happen next is now between these plot arcs and character arcs, you can now develop the manuscript chapter outline. You now can begin to start the outlining structure process by putting in chapters to the manuscript that will correspond to each of these events you have established for your novel. This is how we are going to begin populating the actual outline of the novel. However, for now we are not going to worry about that just yet. What you need to do first now with structuring your novel is to identify the major plot and character arcs that you have established by now.

Occasionally this is where the author or writer can sometimes run into one or a few different roadblocks in this process. The way to overcome this is to take the time here to really flesh out these characters. A huge help here is actually use artwork that you can find by other creators or artists on the internet, or actually real pictures of people that you think are similar to your character to reference. This really helps just as a reference point here to flesh out the characters a little bit more. You can flesh out more of how your characters are going to be, what their point of view(s) are in the plot arcs, as well as what point of view the reader will have towards those characters. Remember that this is not an exact science by any means, and you will find yourself jumping around between doing a bit of your plot arc, then doing some of your characters arc, and hoping back and forth a bit. Your character and plot arcs will all start to organically grow at this point as you continue to put the time into developing and creating it. This process should help if you ever hit a roadblock you can just stop what you were working at the moment, jump to another character arc or plot arc and start going from there. You can jump around if you need to until specific things make sense to you on how to continue past the roadblock you encountered.

At this point you should really have developed a pretty full cast of characters, and understand what you are trying to do with your plot. The next phase that we are going to be doing for structuring your novel is to dive into the three act structure itself. We are going to now take all that has been established, created, and developed so far, and start to drop in scene placeholders until we have built a structural framework of scenes that will go from the beginning of the novel to the end. Again this is a starting point of the main scene roadmap we can now develop, anything can be changed or added to as we write and create our novel as long as it makes sense and fits into the progression of the plot. Then later we will also cover writing descriptions for each of the chapters that will be outlined. This will allow us to really see the final real structure of the plot for the novel.

Chapter 4: The Three Act Structure

Time to dive into the famous Three Act Structure that many writers and successful best selling authors use for the structuring and outlining of their novels. We are going to cover this three act structure now, as well as how you can apply it to your outlining for structuring your novel. Now that you have been through the previous chapters, you can probably see buy now how starting with the outlining process right away is probably not the greatest idea to start with before the other elements are fleshed out a bit more. So far, we have been through establishing that foundational setting that then built into the premise, which then we covered building that into some plot and character arcs already. So by now you should have a pretty good idea of who the cast of characters are in your story, what they are going to need to achieve or work towards throughout the course of the story, and the main plot progression.

Now what we are going to dive into is applying

some more structure to the foundation and information that we current have. We are going to discuss what the famous three act structure is in further detail now since have laid the foundation for it already.

What Is The Three Act Structure?

There are several different types of structures that people apply to stories and novels. The Three Act Structure is one of the most commonly used and prefered story structure methods of many successful and best selling novel authors and writers today. There are a few "literary professors" that may argue that the Three Act Story structure is something used for story structure of screenwriting and not for novel writing based on what they have "studied" and were "taught" in their journey of learning writing. But this is just simply not the case, because the three act structure is really helpful for story structure in general, as well as understanding what makes a great story flow regardless of the platform that particular story is delivered on. This is actually the structure that many best selling fiction novel authors use and teach today as I have previously mentioned. The funny and interesting part about many of these "professors" or "Ph.D's", who have this argument against the three act story structure when it comes to novel writing, is that most all of them have not even written an exceptional novel. Yet if you look at many of the successful and best selling author fiction novelist today this three act structure is what many are using, teaching, and preaching for novel writing, go figure right. Again, there are no hard and fast rules about writing. You do what works well for you, and what you love and enjoy, as well as get the most benefit from, weather that is the three act structure plot driven method, a more character driven method, or any other method. But this three act structure has been so helpful to many authors, as well as myself which is why I recommend it. As an author or writer this structure really helps to give you a great roadmap for your novel and story. It really helps to guide you and keep you as the writer and author from getting lost in your own story. It really helps you to be able to write an effective story very fluidly and efficiently, with much less wasted time, effort, and work by avoiding problems and mistakes.

To take a second to give a bit of history here, the three act structure really dates back to ancient Greek philosophy and Aristotle. This method and structure of storytelling has been iterated over and over again all the way up to the present day. One of the main reasons that many authors and many novel and fiction authors love the three act story structure so much is that it just makes writing and storytelling as a writer so much easier. Lets now cover the basics of how this structure is broken down.

Hence this story structure being called "The Three Act Structure" or "The Three Act Method", there are three separate acts that make up this structure. The first act is the beginning, the second act is the middle, and the third act is the ending. You are going to group all of your scenes for your novel into whatever area or act they fall into in the plot. This is also really going to help you when it comes time to create your outline. Every part of this structure has a few things that are in common from story to story regardless of the genre they come from. You also may remember this breakdown from the "Plot Diagram" that we have already reference and look over in the previous chapter. I recommend referencing those two plot diagrams which I have created, and placed in the previous chapter as needed.

The First Act

In Act one which is also sometimes referred to as "the setup" act, you start with a meaning. This is the point that you are showing your protagonists or leads everyday life and introducing the reader into your world. This is where you can give your protagonist a small problem at first and in fact you should give them a small problem right away. Remember this is their ordinary life and nothing dramatic or too conflicting has occurred just yet. Sometime close to this introduction, you will want to get to the inciting incident or the catalyst in the hero's journey in the plot, or the conflict if call it that. This is where real interruption occurs in the lead's or protagonists life, and they have to figure out dealing with it. This is where you have the chance as an author to show them in action, this is the point as a writer you can show the protagonist doing something that makes the reader root for them because it shows that they are willing to take action and that they are competent. As your lead or protagonist progresses through the first scene you want to now be building towards the first "gateway" or "doorway" into the next act. Each of the three acts in this structure have a "gateway" which is the transition point from one act into the other, some refer to this as the act "doorway" as well as "gateway" which will take the story plot into the next act.

The "inciting incident" is the moment in which you know that the protagonists life cannot go back to the way it was before. One example of this would be if our main lead or hero had their home kingdom or village completely destroyed by the antagonist or forces of the antagonist which causes a complete shift in the plot, and now for the lead there is no going home. The protagonist is at a point of no return in the plot since their home has now completely been destroyed, and his or her whole life has now completely been altered. Now the lead has been through the "inciting incident" and now been thrown into the second act of the plot structure. Now it's the middle of the plot story, and he or she has to decide what to do going forward. So you want to have a moment like that in your story structure. Obviously, I'm not saying that you literally need to do exactly what i'm suggestion above in your story. I am more so speaking to the story structure and flow of having that kind of transitional moment for your main lead or protagonist in your novel's story plot.

The first two things that you really need to now define are the inciting incident, and the first gateway that will lead into the second act of your story structure. If you are stuck at all on this, take a look for ideas on concepts that other successful authors in your genre have done in their novels. Again, not so that you can copy them or their work, but just so that you have a reference point that may help you to understand what could and would not work well for your novel. It also might be helpful here to do this using the main novel you chose in the earlier chapter that we discussed as your IP reference novel for a starting point. Just to make sure to provide clarity on the gateway transition into the second act, once the inciting incident has taken place within our story, the story is then officially at the beginning of the second act.

The Second Act

We are now going to go over the elements and structure for the second act. In the second act usually somewhere around the midpoint of the novel or shortly thereafter is where you have a major crisis of something going catastrophically wrong for the protagonist or maybe even a series of crisis's that are ultimately progressing towards the climax and ending of the story plot. This is the point of your story that things look like they are at the worst for your protagonist. Think of this as being the worst point of your novel for your protagonist or lead. The protagonist lead from here is going to steadily climb up from here towards the ultimate climax from this point, getting more intense and gaining more tension in the story as we progress. We refer to this as you have seen in the plot diagram in the previous chapter as the "rising action". The climax is really the height of act two and is really also the gateway that propels the plot into the third and final act.

The way we should look at the climax is really as the crowning glory of the entire story. The climax could be referred to also as the most epic moment of the novel story. This is the point that the entire story and plot has been continually building to the entire time. Therefore the climax should be really massive for the story and plot. This is the greatest moment of intensity of the story as well. The climax really should be the most exciting part of the whole story, as well as the place where all the major conflicts are resolved. Here we really learn the outcome of the aspects of the plot and story, and conflicts that have been building up to this climax moment in the plot. The climax is the moment in the novel where it all comes to a head and the reader gets the answers to the questions they have been seeking after in the story.

Eventually in this story plot the protagonist will reach a point of no return here, and they will experience and go through the climax of the plot. When they go through the climax, this is the moment where they actually go through the second gateway which takes them into the third and final act of the story structure which is the ending act. In which at that point in the story climax, the protagonist will be completely locked into the conflict.

The Third Act

Now that our protagonist as gone through the second act and main story climax, this has now taken the protagonist into the third, final, and ending act. To clarify when the story and plot gets to the point in which the protagonist reaches the main climax of the story, which is at the end of the second act, this is indeed the very gateway that then takes the plot and story now into the third and final act. The climax has occurred, everything and all the conflict has come to a head, and now the plot has been taken into the third act. Now this is the point of the plot and story where we see how everything plays out and resolves from here within this third act. This entails all the events that after the climax occurs that leads to the end of the story, and is referred to as the "falling action". Now in the plot and the story in the third act this leads to everything being resolved and then ending of the story and novel.

Defining Your Story's Three Acts

The work to be done now for your novel is to now define each of the elements of the three acts in your story that we have discussed in this chapter. This is essentially then going to to be used as the first part of your outline, and the outlining process for your novel which will we cover in the next chapter. Once you have done all this prewriting work we have discussed so far in this book, the outline is actually really simple to do. If you remember when we discussed dropping in all the rest of the data from the other plot and character arcs that were created, for outlining your novel, that's what we will be doing. We will also be taking those elements starting with the inciting incident, we will take all the data in each of the arcs and start creating all the rest of the actual scenes in the story and start placing them within the three arc structure where they belong in each chapter heading leading up to the end of the novel. When you are finished with this you will then have the entire structure and outline for your novels plot.

To help you as a reference in regards to act length for your novel, to give you a rough understanding reference for each act's length as compared to the other, that is generally referred to as the 25-50-25 percentage model. Which just means that the first act is generally about 25% of the novel, with the middle and second act being 50% of the novel, and then the third and final act making up the remaining 25%. This is not a hard and fast rule again, and it's up to you as the writer and author to determine how the percentage that works for your story. This just gives you some reference point for the three act length comparison for the story structure model. Some people for their particular story and plot prefer a shorter first act, or even longer last acts depending on how their novels story is

going. These percentages do however give a
rule of thumb reference point of the general
act percentages with the three act structure.

Chapter 5: Structuring Your Scenes

Scenes are the basic building blocks of your entire outline structure. We are going to dive into how to structure your scenes in this chapter. By understanding what needs to go into the creation of each scene, will really help you to develop your novels outline. This is a skill and element that really makes writing so much easier than people think it is. This helps you to have a structure of where you are going with each scene. It gives you a structure for each scene so that when you sit down at your desk to actually write a scene, that process is just so much easier, as well as much faster. We are going to look at a scene as an example, we will look at exactly how to map it out. We will also discuss some of the questions to ask yourself here that will really help, as well as the information that we need before we actually start writing the scene itself.

This is the part now where we are going to use more information from the plot arcs and story structure elements that have already been defined by this point. We are going to use this information we have previously defined to construct the first scene. For this part you will reference what you have defined using the three act structure just like we covered in the last chapter, your inciting incident, the first gateway or doorway, the crisis, the second gateway, and so on.

Now what you need to do is to take all the rest of your written plot arcs, text that you have defined, and you can use this to create a list of other chapters. These chapters are basically all the dots that are going to connect each of those major points along your story structure and plot. Let's dive into discussion the creation of the first scene.

The First Scene

What you need to do now is reference your plot arcs that you developed from your synopsis and premise like we discussed. Use this information to look back now at how you have defined how your novel will begin. The starting point of your protagonist character arcs, as well as the main plot arc beginning is what we are looking at for this first part. If it makes sense for your story as an example, you can look now at your main plot arc that you have defined, look at the beginning point and/or first line of the main plot arc. You can now take that single line and ask yourself these next five questions against that beginning line or a line starting point that you define.

Starting off it is helpful to just use a computer to just easily copy and paste these lines around with the question and write or type it out. Type or write it out with the five questions so that you can easily type the answers to the questions below. At first you may have to do this and type out the five questions every time, but after awhile you may be able to just do it in your head as you get use to this process. Lets cover the five questions now to ask against the main plot arc line that has been defined.

1. Scene goal: What do I need the reader to know at the end of this scene?

2. What emotion(s) am I trying to evoke?

3. Pick your point of view. Who has the most to lose?

4. What is the setting like? What are some good sensory details?

5. How can I further raise the tension?

To cover the first point we are looking at in this scene you have defined from your main plot arc, the goal here is what we are determining in the first question to start. For defining the scene goal ask yourself "what do you need the reader to know by the end of the scene?", meaning what did they learn along the way? What is the important message of the scene that the reader should take from this scene? The reason we are asking this is because you have to make sure that whatever the answer is that it is actually in the scene. If you are ever at the point where you find that the answer is that something does not contribute to the plot, then you cut it out and don't use it. There must be a reason why something is contributing to the plot in your scenes.

For the second questions about what emotions you are trying to evoke, this could be curiosity, jealousy, frustration, joy, dread, anger, or whatever emotions make sense with your scene and starting plot here.

For the third question here for point of view, we are looking at who has the most to lose in this scene. This is where you need to think about your cast of characters for this scene, and just simply ask yourself the question "out of the characters that are apart of this particular scene, which one has the most to lose here base on what is happening in this scene?". This usually means that this character will also exhibit the highest tension within the scene as well.

For the fourth question on the setting, this will depend on your story and your plot but this is where you will clearly define the setting of your scene and what is around the characters in the scene. This can show in the writing of your scene in different ways depending on your writing style. Weather you are very detailed with your descriptions of the setting as a writing and story teller, or have a more economical writing style will depend on how this will show in your scenes. You could generally be more of an economical writer in the sense that you give descriptions of things in ways that gives the reader just enough to get a good sense of the world and setting for the scene, without bogging or slowing things down too much.

We definitely don't want to write a scene in such a way that draws out, and gets bogged down too much with unnecessary detail to where we lose the attention of the reader. The goal here is to keep the reader engaged with our scene, and keep their attention. The minute that you as a writer lose the attention of the reader, this is where they start skipping and skimming the page in an attempt to re-engage their own attention. If the detail is just too much within a scene it can also lead to the reader completely losing attention in the story, which can cause them to put down the book and walk away, which we definitely don't want. You want to be able to give the reader enough to go with for sure that gives them a great picture and reference for the scene, and then you want to allow them to use their own imagination to fill in the rest in their mind. Now this is how I like to approach this portion of the scene structure, but if you find something better that works for your and your story that you enjoy more then do it. The point here is balance, and this will depend a bit on your own writing style as well as how you continue to develop your writing craft with this. These are just some good things to keep in mind and to mention.

For the last portion of the fourth question, balance the descriptions and give enough information, but not too much just as describing above. Then I just look to define and give a few important sensory details which helps to communicate what I want to in the entire scene. So you need to think of, as well as define a few of these before actually writing the scene.

The last and fifth question that you can ask yourself now for your scene is "How can I further raise the tension?". By this point we have a pretty well laid out scene based on the first four questions, and we should know how the scene is going to go at this point. Now with this fifth question you just look at the scene and look for any changes or additions you could potentially make that could further raise the tension in the scene. This could be information that you add in which the character(s) learn, something that happens or occurs within the scene itself. Or it could be some other event itself that would make the scene better. Don't force it too much here, you want it to flow well with the goal for the scene. Again, if what you are thinking of is not something that actually makes sense in which makes the scene better then don't add it, or just think of something else.

Next in the process would be that you would have gone through all the questions and really fleshed out the scene like we just discussed. Write out all the answers to each of the questions for your scene so that you can really flesh that out in your head, and get it down in written form now. Now you have a completed scene in your mind and really understand the goals and direction of the scene as well as all the elements of it that need to come through to the reader. Now that you have this scene structure and goals completely fleshed out in your mind it is going to make the scene writing process so much easier and enjoyable for you. Now it's time to take these answers and everything that has now been defined for this scene and actually start to write the scene out. I hope you experience that "au ha moment" that many writers experience the first time they use this method. The "au ha moment" of how easy and enjoyable it really makes the writing process for many writers and authors. This process really helps to go from ideas that you have for a great novel and story, into actually writing out a great story for your novel. If you are like me you will also find that doing this makes the writing process go so much faster, and helps you get into that writers flow so much easier. The "writers flow" meaning where you are in a writing flow state of truly doing your best work, as well as it just making writing so much more enjoyable.

The Other Scenes

Now that you have completed the first scene from that main plot arc line that you took and selected. You can now go back to the main plot arc since you have completed that first scene, and now just continue down the lines of the main plot elements. You continue down the plot arc line by line for the info that you need to craft each of the scenes, and following the process we covered above for each of the important lines to create the scene structure for it. So follow the exact same process we just covered with each one of them now. In the next chapter we are going to cover how to now also work with all this information to actually outline your novel.

Chapter 6: Creating Your Outline

In this chapter of structuring your novel we are going to cover how to outline your novel using the scenes you have fleshed out as well as your plot arc elements. Now that you have been fleshing out the scenes for your novel using your main plot arc, and are working with that and going through it to define and create the different scenes for your novel's plot. This is really going to help you know to create a basic outline for your novel structure. This is also going to help you discover some of the different chapters you will need to pop into your outline for outlining and structuring your novel. Therefore, now is the time to also go ahead and do this by dropping in any chapters that make sense by placing them into your outline. Here you are working on populating the chapter outline place holders based on what you going through and seeing in your main plot arc and scene structure. This is not where you are necessarily writing out all of your chapters just yet, it's really just putting a placeholder in the outline for each chapter to continue structuring your novel. Then you will pop in the different scenes you have fleshed out by now or even written out into the chapters in which they belong in for your novel.

This is where you can also start to give each chapter a name that fits in your novel story and plot that you like. Remember that you are not locked in by anything and can change things that make sense as you go at anytime, it's your story. So if you are not 100% sure, maybe just put a few ideas for now and move on for chapter titles. At this point you are really still just going through the main plot arc list of the written out plot that you have already written previously, and popping in the chapter and scene placeholders which is now creating your novels outline. This is where you are going to go through each and every bit of your arcs to make sure that each and every bit of it is represented somewhere in one of your scenes. You can populate this information for where it is in the story for your notes, meaning which of the three acts structure those chapters and scenes belong to.

You can now take the time to work on

populating each of the chapters by placing each of your scenes in the chapter in which they need to belong. This is where you really start seeing your outline and the skeletal structure of your novel really start coming together. This should just be a basic outline, not to complex, just a simple basic outline structure. This is the point where once you complete the task we have already discussed, you can actually start writing the chapters of your novel! As you write through your chapters as well, don't be afraid to make changes. When you really start going through the chapters you may discover another different chapter that needs to be added and dropped somewhere else for example, you can just do that to put a chapter placeholder for it for now. Later on you can flesh that out more to really weave it into the main plot and story. This is where your novel is going to continue to grow and evolve organically, as you start outlining your chapter and scenes and start writing your chapters as well.

Chapter 7: The First Chapter

Writing a novel is such an exciting, fun, and great journey as a writer, and it all begins in the first chapter. Since the story and adventure for a reader begins in the very first chapter, it has to be a good one. This is the opportunity we have as the writer to really grip the reader's attention, and pull them into our world and story. In this chapter I want to take a minute to really discuss the first chapter, and how you as the writer must grip and hook the reader right from the beginning. If you don't effectively hook the reader here in the first chapter, then you run the risk of losing them forever. They may put down your novel never to return again. The reader has taken time out of their life to pick up your book, and open it up to the first chapter of your story, and now it is your chance to deliver the experience they are looking for. Now it is your job as the writer to not let them down. This all begins with even the first sentence of your novel in the first chapter. In this chapter we are going to cover some tips to writing an amazing first chapter in your novel that really grips, hooks, and engages your readers.

This is now where you can use the outline for your novel and scenes that you have created to now write the first chapter in your story. The outline you created with the scenes you have defined is going to give you the picture of what is important here in the first scene and chapter. You should know what you really need to write based on your first chapter outline and beginning scene here in order to hook the readers attention. Before we discuss "The Hook" of your novel, let's take a few minutes to cover the first opening line in the first chapter of your novel.

The First Line

The first line is where it all begins, and this is where you have the first opportunity to hook and grip your reader. Therefore, making the first line of your novel is something that you should really craft well and get right. This is where you really want to pull the reader in and grab their attention from the start, as well as peak their curiosity. The goal here is to really use words that will trigger some kind of reaction for the reader. And depending on what your novel, plot, and scene are, this will be different for different novels and genres. Since by this time you will have already fleshed out what this chapter and scene is really all about, and the goals of it. You should actually already have a really good idea of this. Now it is time to take that, and craft an amazing and gripping first line to your novel. Here you can cause the reader to have questions and curiosity based on what you have written in the first line. The very first line of your novel, should grip the reader in such a way that makes them want to read and find out more.

You may come naturally to this and already have this taken care of, but if you find yourself getting stuck here, or not liking what you are coming up with then I have a few suggestions. My first suggestion is to be creative here and using the goal and understanding now where this scene is going, write a first line that will really get the reader asking themselves "that is really interesting, what does that mean?". You want to leave this reader in a place of wanting to know more after they read your first line of the novel. This is not where you are giving anything away of your story, it's really where you are just pulling the reader in and peaking their curiosity.

In addition you can also write out different lines to compare them, and then choose your favorite one. Another helpful tip here is to take a look at the first line of the IP reference novel you defined based on the earlier tasks that we covered in this book. You can also look at other novels that are in your genre and that are somewhat similar to your story or setting in some way or another. This can help to peak your imagination and understanding of what makes a great first line in a novel. Using your fleshed out scene, and chapter, as well as these tips, and studying other successful authors first lines, I am sure you will be able to craft one that you really love and is unique to you and your novel's story. Now let's discuss The Hook for your novel.

A Strong Hook

The Hook is the very first scene or sequence of

your novel which is really the first chapter of your story. Just like we discussed with the first line of your novel, in the first chapter it is vital that you hook the reader's attention in a way that grips them to continuing reading. You want this hook to be strong enough to cause the reader to keep reading past the first chapter. Just as your first line had this effect to cause them to keep reading the first chapter, the first chapter needs to have a strong hook that will cause them to read the second chapter, and beyond. Again, now that you already know what your first chapter and scene should consist of base on all that you have written and established already for your first chapter, you will have a much easier time doing this effectively.

To give just a few examples of this hook it can be things like how you introduce your protagonist into the first scene, as well as the curiosity and questions that peaks in the reader. You can establish the protagonists everyday life in a way that again causes the reader to want to know more. Then you can introduce a small everyday conflict or problem that the protagonist needs to solve which grips the reader making them want to keep reading to find out what happens. These are just a few examples but may help you in crafting "The Hook" for your first scene and chapter. Remember that this must fit into what you have already fleshed out for the first scene and chapter based on what we have already covered.

This is a great opportunity as the writer to also show more of the protagonist's personality, their shortcomings, their hopes and dreams, and so on. Just like we discussed in regards to the first line of your novel, you can also reference other successful novels in your genre that have similar story elements to yours. Again, not to copy them by any means, but to study them and understand how the author is hooking their readers well in the first scene and chapter. This can be helpful to maybe spark new ideas that help you in writing out your first scene. Remember the real goal here is just that by the end of the first scene and chapter you leave the reader in a place of wanting to know and read more.

Another suggestion that you could try only if you want to is to have someone else, like a friend, or family member who you trust to give you honest feedback. You could ask them to read your first line, chapter, and scene to give you feedback. You can ask them, does this first line as well as first chapter peak their curiosity and leave them dying or at least wanting to know more and keep reading. If you decide to do this, this is where you really want to choose someone who actually reads or enjoys similar setting books within the genre that your novel is in.

Chapter 8: Keys to a Strong Climax

Everything in your novel's story from the very beginning is steadily progressing towards the climax and ending and the third and final act. When the reader gets to the climax we as the writer need to make sure that we deliver here. There is nothing worse than an entire novel story that has progressively built up to the climax through the story plot in a great way, that ends up to have the climax be terrible or anti-climactic for the reader. This is when the reader just feels upset, and like the writer as really just wasted their time. We want to make sure that we avoid this scenario for our novel's plot climax.

There is also nothing as rewarding to the reader as when they are so invested in a novel that continually builds up to the climax and ending, then to have a climax that over delivers. As the reader you are hoping for that epic or amazing ending to the conflict(s) in which the plot has been building up to. This is a key moment in which we have the opportunity as the writer to shine bright for our stories and readers, or fail miserably and make our readers want to thrown our novels in the trash bin. Let's go with the first option of the two, and make sure we create a very strong climax for our novel's that our readers, as well as we ourselves will love.

Remember from our three act structure that the climax occurs at the ending of the second act, and is the gateway, or doorway into the third and final ending act. Like we discussed in that earlier chapter the climax is the crowning glory of the entire plot story. Everything in our story and plot has been building up to this very moment, this is it, it is time. This is where everything comes to a head, and should be the most exciting and greatest moment of intensity of the entire story as well. Since the entire plot and story have been building up to this moment in the novel, the climax needs to be really hard, and really impactful.

Some writers have a real hard time with this part of the story, after they have invested so much into building up to this point now they have to deliver for their story in a huge way. This is one of those biggest, and most important moments for the writer as well. This can cause roadblocks, stress, and anxiety for the writer in which they really can encounter a hard time, or roadblocks when writing their plot's climax. Don't stress here, take a deep breath, we are going to approach this by breaking it down into key elements we need to do in order to create and write a phenomenal crowning glory climax. I want you to know that can and will do this, and you will be able to deliver an amazing climax for your story and reader. I also want to give you permission as the writer to not publish or finish your book until you are one hundred and ten percent happy with it, and in love with your climax yourself. Because if you don't love your story, climax, and ending, then you cannot expect the reader to love it. Let's look at the keys for creating and writing an amazing climax.

Follow The Scene Structure

Remember in writing your climax to first

break it down and write it out by following the exact process we already covered in this book for the climax scene. If you do that you will know what is happening in your climax scene and chapter. You will know it's goal and what is needed to be communicated to the reader through those events. By following this you will know the emotions and resolutions that the climax scene will need to evoke. Make sure to follow the process here for scene structure work that we have already done for all the other scenes and chapters, as this will help you to write what you are intending to. You can then use that fleshed out scene information to write the final version of your climax. But make sure that it is crystal clear in your mind for this scene, with all the scene structure elements that we have already covered.

The Keys To A Strong Climax

Lets now dive into discussing the keys to a strong climax. The climax remember is suppose to be intense, one key is to really give your protagonist a disadvantage here in order to increase the intensity of the scene. Nothing really makes the climax more intense then when the protagonist is at a big disadvantage in the scene. You want the reader to legitimately question here weather the protagonist or lead is going to succeed or not. If the reader feels like the protagonist for sure has no problem, and is certain that they will be just fine for sure, then the climax is really not going to be that exciting. A good tip is to maybe have your protagonist enter into this climax as the expected looser from the disadvantage they are in with the plot and antagonist senario. If you are wondering, yes this indeed can tie into most all fiction genres whether it's war, fantasy, sci-fi, romance, and so on. You really want to begin that tension fast in the climax, because you want your reader really be interested and engaged in your climax from the moment it begins, until the moment it ends.

The Antagonist In The Climax

For the second key to a strong climax, this comes down to the antagonist being bad or evil and really creating that emotion in the reader of seeing how bad or evil the antagonist really is. By this point you really want the antagonist to be lethal, and at the peak point of their evilness and/or darkness. If you don't have a character antagonist for your novel plot, and it is more of a thing, or famine, or some kind of evil, bad, or negative event then really the same concept still applies. This is the climax and you need to make it as bad, terrible, and as big of an obstacle or event that it really needs to be to capture the level of tension and excitement needed for the climax.

There is nothing worse for the reader then to get to the climax of the story just to have an antagonist climax scene where they basically just fall over and die without any unexpected turn, or not have real struggle and difficulty for the protagonist. If your reader is not intimidated by the the antagonist, the bad obstacle, event, or whatever you are using as the antagonist role in your novel, then you are doing it wrong here as the writer. You cannot let the reader down here if you want them to enjoy your novel, and potentially want to read more of your novels. You want to end on a high note and create a raving fan base for your stories, and this is a place you need to shine for your readers. Not living upto the expectations and desires of the reader, will be detrimental for the story. This is where your antagonist really needs to be better and more intense than ever. So make sure to get this scene right, with the correct level of difficulty, excitement, and tension, especially also when it comes to the antagonist. Follow the questions we have discussed in the previous chapters, such as, "how can I raise the tension even more?", and "how can I make this climax even more exciting?".

The Protagonist In The Climax

In the climax for your protagonist, this needs to be a big moment for them like we mentioned. In the climax it is important that this is a big hardship and struggle for the protagonist in which they actually come very close to failing. Again, one thing that would really make for a poor climax is having your protagonist stroll in to the scene like superman versus an antagonist that has no chance, who then is simply defeated or taken care of. This would apply if your antagonist is not actually a character like we were saying as well, like if it were something else like an event or something. This is assuming that you are writing your plot where the protagonist ultimately succeeds, if the protagonist ultimately fails with the story and plot of your novel, then the same concept still applies. Make sure you really manage that scene tension and difficulty here well for the main point with this.

Climaxes where the protagonist almost dies or almost loses are simply more powerful and more enjoyable for the reader, and the readers respond to them, and usually like them so much more. There have actually been plenty of studies that really look at this to prove it with storytelling and plot climax. Readers want to see the protagonist really grow and struggle, and push themselves through to the end. This makes the perseverance of the protagonist really inspiring for the reader, and really helps to build that emotional connection even stronger between the reader and the protagonist.

Surprising The Reader

The fourth element we are going to discuss for some keys of making a great climax is the element of surprise. Try and include elements and/or outcomes in the climax that really surprise or even shock the reader. Not all novels include surprises or plot twists in the climax, however if you are going to surprise the reader the climax is a great place to do it. A great surprise or plot twist really can make the climax that much more exciting and enjoyable for the reader. Such as if the reader is expecting something to happen, but then you completely shock and surprise them with a big twist or surprise. If this is a route that you take in your climax this is where you want to put the reader in the place of gasping out loud, or even causing them to yell "what!?" at their book. If you can accomplish this well, then it can be a wonderful addition to the climax. There are so many ways that you can surprise your reader and this part is really up to you as the writer to determine what makes sense in your plot and story structure. With what you have fleshed out already, for your ending scene you should have a really good idea of this and these elements. However, never be afraid to make changes that just make sense and fit in. If you suddenly have an amazing idea for your climax that just really works well then go for it. Remember that ultimately you are not locked into anything if it makes sense with the plot and story flow until you actually publish your novel. This is where you can get really creative as the writer to provide a really engaging climax to the reader.

Making The Climax Intense

The last thing I want to mention about keys to

a good climax is to remember as the writer that this is the most anticipated part of the entire book and story for the reader. The climax does not have to be the readers favorite part of your novel, but it does need to be the most intense. Something good to do here is to take a look back at other exciting moments in your novel and plot that have already occurred, and try to surpass those with intensity and excitement at least. You may try and surpass your previous exciting moments in your novel with the surprise shock element if that fits into your story well. Remember to do what your ultimately love and enjoy for your story, and do not force things that ultimately don't work. I just took the time to cover a few climax keys here for you, that may help but remember to mainly reference and use your outline, and scene structure elements that you should have fleshed out by this point. Your outline and scene structure is used as the foundation for writing the climax to your plot and story, and it should really help you in writing an outstanding climax.

Chapter 9: The Plot Resolution

I am going to take some time in this chapter to discuss ending your book, which is considered the "falling action" and then the "resolution" ending in the three act structure. You may remember this and seeing it in the plot diagram that we covered earlier in this book. This is the point where the main climax has already occured, we know the results and outcome from this which took us into the third and final act. The third and final act is considered the ending and wrapping up of the main plot. Now is the time to tie up all the unresolved plot threads for your novel. This means all of your subplots as well will need to be address and everything needs to tie neatly together to wrap up the story. The reader should not be left with any major questions at the end, and this definitely also applies to books with sequels. In essence every book must be able to stand by itself as a complete story, even if it is apart of a series.

Make sure you also address and tie up any loose ties with your character arcs as well to get each character in your novel to their proper ending place for the plot of your novel. The character arcs are definitely something that is really helpful to pay attention to for your final scene, this will help to make sure that each character is really ending the story the way they need to be.

You can also write the ending where you add elements to the ending that may powerfully call back to something in the beginning. Again, this all depends on your story, plot, subplots, and character arcs you have developed as to what will make the most sense for your novel. This ending is resolution is really considered the last scene of the novel, and is going to need to be fleshed out just like we have with all the others. I do however want to mention, there maybe a few things that are left open, and that is okay as long as it just makes sense with the ending of your story. As long as the reader has received enough other closer for things that still make up a great ending, even if there are a few loose ends, that make sense for the plot resolution, or if a series, then this may work just fine. This can also be the case to still have some open elements if the story is continuing into a series of novels, just make sure that each novel and ending can stand on its own feet. If a part of a series you just want to make sure each book does give a great climax and ending on it's own for the reader.

I want to just share a question with you that can really sometimes with making sure that you are conveying to the reader what you are intending to as the writer with your ending. This question is, "what emotions do I want to leave my readers with?", or "what emotions do I want my readers to have when they close the end of the book?". This can help you check and make sure you are ending the book for the reader the way that you are meaning, and desiring to.

This is however your novel, your story, your journey as a writer, and your adventure. I cover everything in this book of structuring your novel in hopes that I can really help give you tools to equip and help make that whole journey of writing your novel easier, more effective, as well as more enjoyable for you as the writer. However, remember that your plans may change as your story evolves, and you may have need to change a few things, or even major things in your plot and story as you go. If you have to change some things as you go feel the freedom to do that, that is the great part of being the writer of your world and novel, that you have the complete freedom to do that. Take the tools that I have discussed in this book, use them, apply what is really helpful and enjoyable for you, and discard any that just don't work for you. However, I really encourage you to really try them all first, and give them a really good effort. Ultimately remember that you have the liberty and complete freedom to change things as you go if they make sense to you and your story, and that is totally ok.

I really hope that you have enjoyed this book, and have really been equipped with some great tools for structuring your novel. Now is the time to go write, and create the world in which your future readers don't yet know they are longing to read.

From The Author

If you have enjoyed this book I want to ask you to please do me a favor by leaving a review of this book on the Amazon website book page. Thank you for your support!

Also make sure to claim your free bonus guide on how to write outstanding character's for your novel. I have this as a gift to you for purchasing this book.

GET YOUR FREE COPY OF THIS THREE STEP GUIDE HERE AT THIS BELOW ADDRESS:
www.bit.ly/Claim-My-Free-Guide

Conclusion

I want to personally thank you once again for purchasing this book, Structuring Your Novel. I really hope that you have enjoyed it and that it has provided some great value to you.

The methods covered in Structuring You Novel might have sounded intimidating, but now that you know everything about it, just start from the beginning and take one step at a time. I encourage you to really try these methods with your best effort to truly discover which methods work really well for you, and your writing process.

This book has provided you with the information that you really need to know about how to structure and outline your story to write an exceptional novel. These methods will help you to make the whole writing process easier, faster, better, more enjoyable, and more liberating. I suggest that you really try to implement these techniques with consistent effort over a period of time to really hone in your craft as what will work best for you.

If you have enjoyed this book I ask that you would please consider leaving a review on Amazon for this book to let me know, and I wish you all the best on your journey of Structuring Your Novel. Thank you, and I wish you all the best on your Structuring Your Novel and writing journey!

Copyright

warranties of any kind are expressed or implied. Readers acknowledge that the author is not engaging in the rendering of legal, financial, medical or professional advice. The content of this book has been derived from various sources. Please consult a licensed professional before attempting any techniques outlined in this book.

By reading this document, the reader agrees that under no circumstances are is the author responsible for any losses, direct or indirect, which are incurred as a result of the use of information contained within this document, including, but not limited to, —errors, omissions, or inaccuracies.

www.ingramcontent.com/pod-product-compliance
Lightning Source LLC
Chambersburg PA
CBHW050035260726
48658CB00005B/1611